Capybaras AND Pygmy Mice

Henry Thatcher

PowerKiDS press.

New York

Published in 2014 by The Rosen Publishing Group, Inc.
29 East 21st Street, New York, NY 10010

First Edition

Produced for Rosen by Cyan Candy, LLC
Editor: Joshua Shadowens
Designer: Erica Clendening, Cyan Candy

Photo Credits: All images Shutterstock.com, except p. 11 Stefan Dressler, via Wikimedia Commons;
pp. 22, 24, 29 Wikimedia Commons.

Library of Congress Cataloging-in-Publication Data

Thatcher, Henry, author.
 Capybaras and pygmy mice / by Henry Thatcher. — First edition.
    pages cm. — (Big animals, small animals)
 Includes index.
 ISBN 978-1-4777-6114-4 (library) — ISBN 978-1-4777-6115-1 (pbk.) —
 ISBN 978-1-4777-6116-8 (6-pack)
 1. Capybara—Juvenile literature. 2. Pygmy mice—Juvenile literature. 3. Rodents—Juvenile
 literature. I. Title.
 QL737.R662T43 2014
 599.35—dc23

                             2013023453

Manufactured in the United States of America

CPSIA Compliance Information: Batch #W14PK2: For Further Information contact Rosen Publishing, New York, New York at 1-800-237-9932.

Table of Contents

Rodents, Big AND Small

Rodents make up one of the most plentiful orders of **mammals** on Earth. In fact, forty percent of all mammals are rodents. Rodents include animals such as mice, rats, squirrels, beavers, guinea pigs, and hamsters. You might think all rodents are small mammals. You have never seen a capybara, then! Capybaras are the largest rodents in the world. They can be nearly 4.5 feet (1.3 m) long and 2 feet (.6 m) at the shoulder.

There are around 2,277 rodent species in the world.

4

Next to the capybara, the pygmy mouse looks tiny. Next to any mammal the pygmy mouse looks tiny, though! These mice are some of the smallest rodents, and smallest mammals, in the world. These mice are generally between 1 and 3 inches (30–80 mm) long.

PYGMY MOUSE

Where IN THE World?

Capybaras live in South America and some parts of Central America. They live in parts of every country in South America except Chile.

The African pygmy mouse makes its home in sub-Saharan Africa. The desert pygmy mouse lives in Angola, Botswana, Namibia, South Africa, Zambia, and Zimbabwe. The Free State pygmy mouse, or orange mouse, lives in Lesotho and South Africa. Setzer's pygmy mouse lives in Botswana, Namibia, and Zambia. Thomas's pygmy mouse and the gray-bellied pygmy mouse live in Angola,

Here is a male capybara with his children, in Venezuela, South America.

Cameroon, Republic of the Congo, Democratic Republic of the Congo, Gabon, Kenya, Rwanda, Sudan, Tanzania, and Uganda.

There are also **species** of pygmy mice that live in North America, in Mexico, Arizona, New Mexico, Texas, and Oklahoma. The southern pygmy mouse lives in El Salvador, Guatemala, Honduras, Mexico, and Nicaragua.

At Home IN THE Water AND IN THE Fields

Capybaras' scientific name is *Hydrochoerus*, which means "water pig." This is in part due to how this rodent looks, but is mostly due to the **habitat** it prefers. Capybaras live along riverbanks, beside ponds, or in marshes. They will live anywhere there is standing water available. Sometimes this can be on savannas or in dense forests. They have feet that are partly webbed and spend much of their time in the water. Capybaras are closely related to agoutis, chinchillas, coypus, rock cavies, and guinea pigs.

The lesser capybara is a species of capybara that lives in eastern Panama, northwest Colombia, and western

Capybaras are excellent swimmers and spend a lot of time in and near the water.

Venezuela. Lesser capybaras are about half the size of normal capybaras. It also chooses homes where there is water in which to swim, find food, and hide from danger.

BERRY

The northern pygmy mouse lives in coastal prairies and prairies further inland. They will live in desert shrublands, in the grasses around prickly pears, and in mixed forests. They prefer dense ground cover to be available in all of these habitats.

A typical savanna where pygmy mice live in Burkina Faso, Africa.

The African pygmy mouse lives in grasslands and savannas south of the Sahara desert. The grasses provide food and also help them hide from **predators**. Pygmy mice are just the right size to make a nice snack for all kinds of animals. Lucky for them, their small size and coloring make them hard to spot in their grassy habitats.

How Are They Alike?

At first glance, capybaras and pygmy mice seem pretty different. Capybaras weigh as much as an adult person, where as pygmy mice weigh less than a "fun-sized" chocolate bar. Capybaras look something like furry pigs or beavers without tails. Pygmy mice look a lot like house mice.

This small mouse is nibbling on a piece of wood.

However, size aside, they have many features in common. First of all, both animals are rodents. This means they have two front pairs of gnawing teeth that never stop growing. In fact, the name rodent comes from the Latin word *rodere* meaning "to gnaw," or "to chew." They must chew to keep these teeth short. Rodents use their teeth to gnaw on wood, break open seeds or other foods, and to bite predators in defense.

Here a capybara walks along a riverbank looking for food.

These animals are also mammals with fur-covered bodies. As with all mammals, they give birth to live babies and feed those babies with milk made by the females' bodies.

Two adult, and one young, capybara are going for a swim.

They both tend to like grassland habitats. However, the capybaras live mainly in South America. Pygmy mice live in Africa or in parts of Central and North America. Pygmy mice are great at climbing. Capybaras are better at swimming than they are at climbing. Most species of rodents are plant-eaters, though some eat insects, birds, worms, or fish.

Comparing CAPYBARAS

Size .... 4.5 feet (1.3 m) long; 2 feet (0.6 m) at the shoulder

Habitat.............. forests, savannas, and near water

Diet................... herbivores

Predators .... big cats and people

Prey.................. none

Life Span........... 8 to 10 years

AND PYGMY MICE

Size .... 1 to 3 inches (30–80 mm) long

Habitat .... grasslands

Diet .... omnivores

Predators .... snakes, birds, skunks, and raccoons

Prey .... occasional insects, snails, and small snakes

Life Span .... around 1 year in the wild

17

One Big Rodent!

Capybaras are highly social. This means they live together in large groups of 10 to 20 animals. Sometimes they can be found in even larger groups of up to 100 capybaras. Most groups have a mix of males, females, and young. There is one **dominant** male in each group. Capybaras make lots of noises to communicate with each other.

Capybaras have reddish-brown fur on the tops of their bodies and yellowish-brown fur on their undersides. Their back legs are slightly longer than their front legs, and their feet are partly webbed. Their back feet have three toes, but their front feet have four. Their footprints look a bit like stars due to the webbing. Like hippos, capybaras have their nostrils, eyes, and ears on top of their heads. This adaptation allows them to stand mostly underwater and still be able to see and breathe.

BIG FACT!

Groundhogs, another rodent, are sometimes called whistle pigs. They whistle for a different reason than capybaras do, though. They whistle to warn of danger.

When it is time to mate, a female will whistle through her nose to let males know she is available. Mating happens in the water. Around 4 to 5 months after mating, females will give birth to around four babies. The mother returns to her group hours after giving birth. The young follow once they

This is a close-up of a mother capybara (Hydrochoerus hydrochaeris) *and two of her babies, in a lake.*

Here two baby capybara sit together among some sticks.

are able to move. Baby capybaras will drink milk from their mothers for about 16 weeks. In fact, they will drink milk from any available female in the group. They start eating grasses after they are about a week old.

As Small AS A Mouse!

The pygmy mouse has reddish or gray fur on top and a white or light gray belly, depending on the species. These tiny mice are close relatives to the house mouse. Pygmy mice are social and like to live in groups with other pygmy mice.

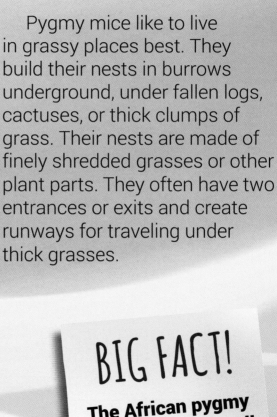

Pygmy mice like to live in grassy places best. They build their nests in burrows underground, under fallen logs, cactuses, or thick clumps of grass. Their nests are made of finely shredded grasses or other plant parts. They often have two entrances or exits and create runways for traveling under thick grasses.

BIG FACT!

The African pygmy mouse builds a wall of pebbles in front of its burrow.

The northern pygmy mouse can mate at nearly any time of year. Just 20 days after mating, females give birth to litters of one to five babies. These tiny babies can fit on a dime! They are born blind and without hair, but they grow quickly. Within two weeks their eyes open, and they stop drinking milk from their mothers by three weeks. They are fully **mature** at two months of age.

Here is a mouse peeking out of its hiding place in the snow. Mice need to hide from their predators.

One of the reasons pygmy mice like to live in places with plenty of cover is that they make a delicious meal for many animals. Some of their main predators are snakes and **nocturnal** birds of prey, such as owls. Coyotes, raccoons, skunks, and shrews will eat pygmy mice, too.

Diets: Big AND Small

Capybaras are **herbivores**, munching on grasses, aquatic plants, fruit, and sometimes tree bark. When food is plentiful, capybaras can be quite choosy. They will eat their favorite leaves of one kind of plant and ignore the rest. However, they will eat whatever is available during the dry season. Plants are not easy to digest, or break down. Capybaras have adapted in a few ways to help get as much nutrition from their food as possible. One way they

The world's largest rodent, the capybara, is nibbling on some grass.

A capybara is caught eating a blade of grass, one of its favorite snacks.

GRASS

do this is by eating their own waste. This sounds gross, but their waste is an important source of bacteria that their stomach needs to break down the tough parts of the plant. Plus, by eating their waste, their stomachs have another chance at getting more protein and vitamins from the plants. Capybaras will also **regurgitate**, or bring their food out of their stomach and back into their mouths. They then chew the food again to break it down further.

27

Pygmy mice are **omnivores**, but they eat mostly plants. They will eat grasses, seeds, and other plants. The northern pygmy mouse eats the stems and fruit of prickly pear

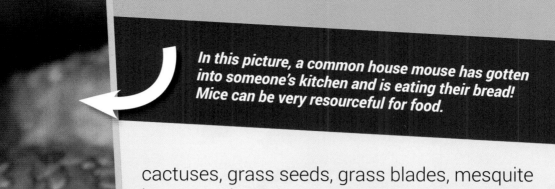

In this picture, a common house mouse has gotten into someone's kitchen and is eating their bread! Mice can be very resourceful for food.

cactuses, grass seeds, grass blades, mesquite beans, and granjero berries. It is thought that the mice also eat insects, snails, and small snakes.

PRICKLY PEAR CACTUS

Big or Small, Does it Matter?

Rodents have done very well for themselves for thousands of years. Nearly half the mammal species on Earth are rodents. Rodents are successful because they are **adaptable**, smart, and able to live near people. Capybaras and pygmy mice are no different. In fact, both these rodents are often kept as pets. Capybaras are known for being highly trainable and loyal pets. Pygmy mice can be hurt if handled but are fun to watch. They are even more fun to learn about in their wild habitats!

Capybaras are raised by people and hunted in the wild for their meat. So far, despite human use of these animals, capybaras are still plentiful in the wild. However, people must be careful that our actions do not hurt animals, both big and small, that share the planet with us.

A capybara follows an American wood stork through some swamp land in South America.

Glossary

adaptable (uh-DAP-tuh-bul) Able to be fit to meet requirements.
dominant (DAH-mih-nent) In charge.
habitat (HA-buh-tat) The kind of land where an animal or a plant naturally lives.
herbivores (ER-buh-vorz) Animals that eat only plants.
mammals (MA-mulz) Warm-blooded animals that have backbones and hair, breathe air, and feed milk to their young.
mature (muh-TOOR) Fully grown.
nocturnal (nok-TUR-nul) Active during the night.
omnivores (OM-nih-vorz) Animals that eat both plants and animals.
predators (PREH-duh-turz) Animals that kill other animals for food.
regurgitate (ree-GUR-juh-tayt) Throw up partly eaten food.
rodents (ROH-dents) Animals with gnawing teeth, such as mice.
species (SPEE-sheez) One kind of living thing. All people are one species.

Index

Websites

Due to the changing nature of Internet links, PowerKids Press has developed an online list of websites related to the subject of this book. This site is updated regularly. Please use this link to access the list:
www.powerkids.com/basa/mice/